For My Sisters:

7 Relationship Tips

by

Thomas Long

ISBN: 0-9715530-1-7

Library of Congress Control Number: 2003090806

Cover Design by: Leigh Woolston Karsch
(website: www.leighwoolston.com)

Back Cover Photo by: Boh Jackson

Published by XSL Publishing, Inc.
Baltimore, Maryland 21215

Printed in the United States by Morris Publishing
3212 East Highway 30
Kearney, NE 68847
1-800-650-7888

Acknowledgements

Thank you's are extended sincerely to the following:

First and foremost to my ***Creator*** for instilling in me the ability to effectively communicate through the use of the written word and for giving me the vision to complete this work; to my family and friends for your undying support and unconditional love; to all of the women that have crossed my path on an intimate level (no names need to be mentioned because you know who you are) for the wealth of useful information and life experiences that you gave to me that have aided me in my research efforts for this topic; to my "editors" in training : J. Hughes, F. Mohamed, S. Perryman, K. Robinson - I know I drove you all crazy asking for your input and criticisms, but it was greatly appreciated; to Mrs. Leigh Woolston Karsch- I appreciate the cover design because it was definitely hot!; to the following bookstores for giving an independent writer a chance to shine with my first book: Sepia, Sands, and Sable (Richard- Baltimore: I appreciate all of your help and advice on the business tip), Everyone's Place (Brother Nati- Baltimore: it was a pleasure to meet the esteemed Haki Madhubuti), Basic Black Books (Lecia- Philadelphia), Nubian Bookstore (Marcus- Atlanta), Medu Bookstore (Nia- Atlanta: thanks for the invite to the Black Book Festival!), and Black Facts Books (Carl Weber- New York: I loved all your books, so keep bringing the drama!); last but not least sincere appreciation and respect is due to all of the beautiful women in the world who have been mistreated and their love taken for granted- you are truly a most precious jewel that God gave to man and once we recognizes this fact, the human family will finally be at peace with one another.

T. Long

Table of Contents

Introduction

Before I get started on the primary content of this book, which is to address building healthy intimate relationships, I would like to first discuss my primary motivation for choosing this topic to write about. This book is a testament to my appreciation and respect for womanhood and the infinite value that women have in contributing to the sustenance of the human family. It reflects my efforts and aspirations to try to stimulate intelligent dialogue about relationship issues that plague young America today. Specifically, my aim is to focus on the female's relationship issues by analyzing what role she can play in improving the current relationship trend among our generation. This book is in no way an effort to bash women because I don't think that I could handle the backlash of their wrath if I were to do so (joke).

In analyzing my own personal intimate relationships, as well as those of other young people I've had the privilege of conversing with over the past few years, there seems to be a lack of understanding and effective communication between males and females in my age group (25-35). It has led to the existence of an epidemic of domestic turmoil between the sexes. It seems as though my generation has no idea what it takes to form healthy relationships with each other. Instead, we see many instances of domestic abuse, infidelity, a general lack of respect for each other, and drama filled adventures that many of us want to call relationships. It's not my intention to step on any toes, but maybe to shed some light of truth that can alleviate some of the strife and tension that is becoming more and more pervasive today in our social interactions with one another.

I believe that women are truly the more compassionate and loving gender naturally, but that many of them have lost touch with this sensitive side of themselves as a result of dealing with negative social situations such as being in dysfunctional intimate relationships. They appear to have lost more of themselves in these relationships than men have. A conscious woman in a healthy relationship can be a man's best friend, lover, and business partner as well as a caring mother to her children. Conversely, a woman that has been through a series of bad relationships can be a man's worst nightmare. Their mental and emotional scars from being in "bad" relationships seems to impede their ability to find new relationships that may be beneficial to them. Instead, many chose to stay in relationships where there is no true happiness to be found on any level. I believe that some of the basic elements of healthy relationship building have gotten lost in the midst of all this madness between the sexes and I would like to make an effort to address this issue.

Although this book is specifically aimed at the female population, it is in no way suggesting that the problems that exist in relationships today are totally endemic to women. To make such an assertion would be a grave fallacy on my part and due them a disservice. We, as men, contribute just as much to the relationship process either being a successful one or a dismal failure. However, most literature that I have read on relationships generally comes from a female point of view and seems slanted towards analyzing the behavioral patterns of men in relationships. With this book, I want to discuss some of the primary issues that I see confront women in relationships from a male's perspective. It's time for a man to step up and add a little balance to this discussion about relationships between the sexes!

Some of the major relationship issues that I want to discuss in this book include dealing with emotional baggage before getting into a relationship, the importance of having shared life goals and interests with your mate, developing an open line of communication with your partner, and having clearly defined roles and responsibilities for each individual within the relationship. In addition, I want to explore some intimacy problems that may develop between the man and woman and what role they may play in either maintaining or dissolving the bond between the two. It is my belief that these issues are at the core of most of the relationship conflict that exists among my generation and that is why I chose them to be the central focus of my work. I plan to go into detail with each topic and explain how each one can have a negative or positive impact on a relationship depending on how they are approached. Also included in the text will be possible solutions or means of resolving these problems so as to reduce conflict and promote harmony between the man and woman as they seek to come into oneness with each other.

Now I know many women may question how a man can dare to suggest to woman what she needs to do to maintain a productive relationship with a man or where she may be going wrong in her current situation to prevent future problems. My response to this is who better than a man that has been in the dating game for years to give advice on what things that a man likes to see in his woman to keep him happy? Not only that, who better than a man with three sisters and a host of female friends that are open in discussing their relationship problems with him to give you a few insightful pointers to aid you in your search for a committed relationship? With that being said, I think that I may be able to make a few relevant points that can be beneficial and informative to my female counterparts as they search for a "soul mate" in the new millennium. I hope you enjoy the reading and take my suggestions to heart in giving them sincere consideration in helping you find and keep that ultimate loving relationship with the man of your dreams.

1

The Bag Lady Syndrome

A serious, intimate relationship between a man and woman requires a strong, emotional commitment from both partners for the relationship to persist. I do not believe that a meaningful, loving bond is created between two individuals as a result of some climatic event or act of fate, but that it is a feeling that evolves after a protracted period of social interaction. A lot of time and energy is invested by both parties during the courtship and dating process that eventually leads up to creating the proper environment for a healthy, monogamous relationship to exist. However, as evidenced by the high rates of divorce and domestic strife that are present in the

American society, things don't always go according to plans and follow the ideal model of a healthy relationship. There are a variety of reasons for the existence of so much relationship conflict in the American society and I plan to discuss just a few of these issues.

During the course of a relationship, many issues tend to arise that may lead to the two going their separate ways, either amicably or in a bitter fashion. Some of these issues include the infidelity of one or both partners, a lack of trust between them, the failure of the two to not clearly establish relationship borders beneficial to each other's personal needs, and unforeseen incompatibility in reference to each individual's personality traits. The chapters proceeding this one will go into further detail in analyzing the significance of these issues to the relationship process. At this time, I want to focus on the impact that carrying around emotional baggage can have on your chances to be involved in a satisfying relationship.

If you notice, most people who say that they fell in love with someone at "first sight" generally wind up in a relationship that is explosive and adventurous initially. However, once the sparks die down, this "love" mysteriously fades away after a short period of time. That is because the attraction which laid the foundation for the relationship was not rooted in anything solid, but was merely a product of infatuation and sexual lust. When a man and woman become involved sexually in the early stages of a relationship without taking the time to get to know each other's character strengths and defects, as well as other similarities and differences, the physical attraction usually fades away after a few months when they both begin to notice the lack of compatibility that really exists between them. Consequently, this love affair is not likely to develop into a long-lasting, healthy relationship.

I believe that the above mentioned situation happens all too often today in relationships. Not enough time is invested by either individual in getting acquainted with their partner's personality before sex comes into play. As a result, many of us wind up sleeping with someone that we hardly even know. In addition, by not adequately knowing much personal information about your sex partner, the door is left open for any number of surprise revelations to arise that could lead to arguments and a parting of the ways between the two of you. For example, he may snore at night or leave the toilet seat up after he uses the bathroom and this may annoy the hell out of you. It doesn't take a lot of time before these little things turn into bigger issues and the heated arguments start to occur. During the break-up period, a lot of things may be said or done out of anger, and not clear thought, that may have a long lasting effect on the psyche of both the male and the female with respect to the manner in which they approach relationships in the future.

In these relationships that end on a sour note, it is my belief that the woman suffers the greatest emotional loss. I say this because women seem to place a stronger emotional attachment to their actions and level of commitment in a relationship than men do (sorry fellas!). As a result, they are left worse off in these situations. For example, most men can have sex with a woman and see it as another sexual conquest with no strings attached. Conversely, a woman tends to see having sex with a man as sharing a special part of herself with someone that she believes may become a potential boyfriend or husband. I'm not in anyway saying that there are no women who have casual sex, but I don't think that the desire is as prevalent among women as it is among men. I think that most women do want to be in a committed relationship, but some have become so frustrated with their inability to find the right man that they will settle for having meaningless sexual interludes as a substitute for love.

When a woman feels as though she has given her heart and soul to a man and he does something negative to end that relationship, she, more often than not, has a tendency to feel vengeance and anger towards him and, possibly, all other men. This rage is not an uncommon feeling for not just women, but for anyone who feels as though they have been treated unjustly in a situation involving someone else's malicious actions. However, how we effectively deal with this rage determines what impact this event may have on altering our lives in a negative or positive way.

In today's society, it seems as though many women who have been through a series of "bad" relationships want to cling to the popular notion that all men are "dogs" and not capable of being in committed relationships. This is a false assumption based on their own past bad experiences with certain men, but many seem to feed into this way of thinking and use it as a springboard to project their inner hostility towards any possible future love interests. I call this the "Bag Lady Syndrome," which the singer, Erykah Badu, discusses in her hit song by the same name.

In the song, "Bag Lady", Erykah Badu gives us a picture of a woman who carries around the emotional baggage of her negative life experiences and who appears to have lost a large piece of her self-identity in the process. I argue that this is the mentality that many women possess today as a result of being in unhealthy relationships. Many women have chosen to define themselves through their mates, and when he is no longer a part of their lives, they are left emotionally and socially displaced. They seem to place doing things to please their mate above pursuing their personal happiness and life's goals. They tend to isolate themselves from their female friends in an effort to show their level of commitment to their relationship.

These are just two examples of the grave mistakes that I found that many women make in a relationship that, in the end, work against them. I say this because once you cut your friends off to be with a man and the relationship doesn't work out, you are lucky if your friends want to accept you back into their company. Then you may truly find yourself isolated, depressed, and angry with your ex because you feel as though he is the cause of you separating yourself from your friends. However, in reality, you should be angry with yourself because it was your decision to make the choices that you made. Please don't forget that relationships are subject to end at any moment, but a friendship is something that should be cherished as being a lifelong union.

That old saying "hell hath no fury like a woman scorned" is accurate to describe the emotional backlash that occurs when a woman is heartbroken by what she perceives to be a "no good" man. Expect for her to rear her horns and spew venom at any man that comes her way for a good while. None of us like to waste our time on something that is worthless or not beneficial to our personal growth, but this is exactly how a woman is left feeling after a break-up on bad terms. I certainly wouldn't want to be in the path of this woman when she starts to vent.

I would strongly urge any woman to address her personal issues with respect to her anger before becoming involved with another man. I say this because getting into a new relationship without bringing closure to a past situation can have drastic consequences. A relationship that begins while one person is on the "rebound" from someone else generally leads to an innocent bystander being hurt in the process. No man wants to be second place in a woman's life to a past lover. If you still have feelings for your ex, it will show in time to this new person. It doesn't take a man being a rocket scientist for him to figure out that you're not really interested in him and that you are just using him as a way to fill an emotional void in your life.

It is equally wrong to project your own personal pain and suffering onto another innocent person for the selfish reason of venting your hurt, but many women resort to this tactic. Some women will date a man who is really a nice guy and just treat him bad because they think they're getting back at their old flame. However, in reality, they're not hurting anyone but themselves. I always subscribe to the belief that what we do wrong today will always come back to haunt us at a later date. So ladies keep this in mind when you want to "dog" a man for your own personal amusement or as a way to lash out at him for another man's wrongdoings.

I would strongly suggest that you take time out to be alone after getting out of a bad relationship to adequately heal your emotions and thoughts. Get away from the dating scene for a while and explore many of the positive attributes within you that may have been forgotten as a result of this negative episode in your life. If you don't, you'll only wind up repeating the same bad cycle that you've been trapped in for so long going from relationship to relationship. Do a thorough self-evaluation and get to know you again as the positive individual you were created to be. A good cleansing of the soul and spirit is always healthy when you want to make a fresh start in life.

In doing a thorough self-evaluation in this rediscovery period, be open and honest with yourself in acknowledging your true feelings for your ex. Don't be dishonest with yourself in thinking that just because the relationship ended, so did your emotional bond to that person. This only leaves the door open for him to remain a factor in your life. No matter what they've done wrong, the ones we love will always be a part of us because they've played a part in our growth and development. However, it is up to you to define what role he will play in your future as you move on to new experiences in life. If after stepping back and evaluating the relationship you see that the bad times outweighed the good, this makes it easier for you to let those bitter feelings go and make your healing process go along smoother.

Another tip I would like to suggest is to find a list of new social activities to be involved in as a form of relaxation and stress management. Come up with new hobbies to keep you busy and productive during this period. Refocus your energy on the things in life that make you happy and clear your mind of negative thoughts. I would recommend a week's vacation on a tropical island either alone or with friends as an excellent getaway to recuperate. Use this time as a chance to mend fences with your girlfriends. Whatever you choose to do, just remember that this is a time for you to open new avenues in your life so let your imagination run wild, but not crazy!

Once you have taken the time to throw off the emotional baggage of the past and are a healthy, refreshed woman, you are now ready to re-enter the dating scene. I would like to make a few suggestions to you to use as a guide in choosing a new mate. First of all, open, honest communication is important to a healthy relationship getting off on the right foot. While you are in the process of getting to know someone new, be honest in discussing with him the relationship experiences you have had in the past to give him an understanding of the boundaries you plan to set in any future relationships. Clearly outline your expectations and aspirations so that there are no misunderstandings between the two of you over unnecessary things. This will allow him an opportunity to see where you stand on specific relationship issues and you can see where he stands so that you both can decide if there is an adequate enough level of compatibility there for you to continue dating.

Secondly, be sure not to make comparisons between this new person and your ex. This is unfair to him because all men are not the same and this one may truly have your best interest at heart. Judge him as an individual and according to his actions not those of your ex because they are two different people. Don't let your inability to move on past your ex make you miss out on a good opportunity to get to know someone who may bring happiness into your life. At the same time, be cautious to recognize any situations or things he may do that you take issue with and be quick to point them out to him in a tasteful manner. This brings us back to the idea that having an open door of communication with your partner is vital to healthy relationship building.

A third and final suggestion I want to make is that if you do get involved in a new relationship, don't be upset if it doesn't work out. Every relationship we are a part of in our lives is not going to be the right one for us and we must accept this reality. In fact, a failed relationship should be looked at as a learning experience and taken as a guide to improve your ability to form healthier relationships in the future. Be sure not to fall back on old habits of holding resentment and anger towards all men. Pick yourself back up and get back into the dating game because you are bound to find someone that you have a lot of things in common with and who is ready for a committed, one on one relationship.

When you do find that one, don't be afraid to put your all into making things work. We get what we give in life and if you give only a half effort to your partner, expect to receive the same in return. You can't be afraid to show your emotions again to a man because that will only lock you into living a lonely existence. There is someone out there for everyone so just keep searching until you find him or he finds you.

Keep these things in mind and you can avoid the trap that many women have repeatedly fallen into time after time not being able to move on with their lives because of the past. Remember that this is a new day, time for a new man, and more importantly, a new you! Appreciate the fact that you have been able to regain your self-respect and hold your head up high as a proud woman as you begin a new chapter in your life. Baggage from the past will only weigh you down and leave you with burdens too heavy for your delicate shoulders to carry.

Discussion Notes

2

A Vision Shared

In choosing a mate, one of the first things you should look for in a man is the potential for personal and social growth. He should have a clearly defined list of short-term life goals, leading up to a bigger plan, which you can visibly see him working towards achieving. For example, if he discusses with you that he is in the process of starting his own business or attending college to pursue his life long ambition to be a lawyer, look for signs in his actions, and not just his words, that suggest that his intentions are legitimate. A clearly, outlined business plan or long hours studying his coursework are good indicators that you may have come across a man that's focused on obtaining success in life. I am a firm believer in the old idea that "if a man fails to plan, he plans to fail." The man who has a vision and follows a step-by-step program to fulfill this vision is the type of individual you should want in your life to complement you as a helpmate.

Going even further, it is important to recognize the difference between a man who has realistic, attainable goals as opposed to one who has set his sights on achieving goals in life that are somewhat far fetched and highly unlikely for him to accomplish. Take, for instance, the man who has had the dream of being a professional singer since he was a child and this is the only goal he is pursuing in his life. He has no steady job or income to fall back on, but merely exists off of the charity of others for his sustenance. This is the type of individual you should strongly consider not becoming involved with in an intimate relationship. I'm not saying that he may not one day become a professional singer or that he should give up on his dream, but given the level of competition and the politics involved in the entertainment industry, his chances are slim. Don't get yourself caught up in a situation where you find yourself putting your life plans on hold to aid someone who is not on a level playing field with you professionally. This will only lead you down a road of misery and heartache and possibly make you lose focus on what you are trying to achieve in your life.

Two things that I have learned in my life are

that we should never put all of our eggs in one basket and that a good back-up plan always comes in handy. Songwriting and writing poetry have always been passions of mine which I wanted to pursue professionally, but I also realized that as a responsible adult, I had bills to pay and I couldn't wait on a "mystery" God to pay them for me. That is why I made sure that I got myself a good education and found stable employment to be able to provide for myself while I pursued my writing aspirations in my spare time. No conscious man should want to be a burden on someone else, financially or otherwise, when he is fully capable, both physically and mentally, of taking care of his own personal needs. Having independence is an invaluable asset for any self-respecting human being and is something we should all strive towards obtaining.

When you see a man working in a systematic manner towards achieving something in life, it says something about his character and personality. For one, it says that he is self-motivated and possesses a certain amount of self-discipline that may be beneficial to you as a support system in your career pursuits. Secondly, it says that he is career-oriented and has the potential to bring as much to the table, both financially and socially, as you are able to provide. A third and final statement that his actions suggest about him is that he has some form of structure and stability in his life. I'll elaborate further a little later as to why this is an important factor to consider as you enter into a relationship with someone. All of these factors add up to positive character attributes that you should look for in a man, but we both know that our eyes and hearts have a way of leading us to being attracted to individuals that are not always beneficial to our life's plans.

Many women I've encountered in my travels have gotten themselves stuck in relationships with individuals who are not on the same career path as they are, but instead are still in the "finding themselves" stage of their lives. I've seen many professional, career-oriented women with a mate who is either "in between" jobs or merely content staying at home living off of his women's generosity. In addition, I've met many more who are attracted to the thug-type of male that has no long-term plans for the future, but lives just for the present day and time. I find it interesting that so many intelligent and apparently well-educated women choose to settle for this type of man to be their "soul mate". In the long run, he turns out to be more of a hindrance as opposed to being a helper in their pursuit of success in life. After speaking to many of them about this issue, I was somewhat shocked by the responses I received.

Many of the women I've talked with stated that they chose to get involved with their mate despite his employment status (or lack thereof) because they believed in his potential. They sincerely believe that they can "change" this non-productive man into a model of success with their guidance and support. The sad reality is that no woman, no matter how much she loves her man, can motivate a man to do anything in life that he does not have the motivation within himself to do. I would also argue that women possess a natural, maternal instinct that makes them want to nurse their "sick puppy" back to health to get him back on his feet. However, a manipulative male uses this inherent characteristic that women have been endowed with against them all the time.

Instead of their helpfulness aiding the man to do better in life, it generally produces the direct opposite response from its original intent. Their partner becomes more lackadaisical and entrenched in his amotivational behavior and sees no reason to get a job as long as his women is willing to take care of him. These types of relationships usually end up in conflict because when the women finally wakes up to the reality that she can no longer play the role of her man's "mother," she begins to feel used and manipulated. No woman can be satisfied forever in a relationship where she does all of the giving and no receiving. A relationship should be a reciprocal situation and when it's not, don't expect for it to last long or end peacefully.

In reference to the women that's attracted to the "thugged-out" man, her fate in relationships is generally the same as her predecessor above. I found in my research that many women who are attracted to the "rough-looking" male choose this type of man because he represents the direct opposite of the type of home environment in which they were raised. This type of female generally comes from a stable home environment and has a "good" family background. Conversely, the thug comes from the rough side of the street culture and was usually raised in a household where there was little or no discipline for him. His morals and values embody everything that her parents worked so hard to keep her away from for most of her life. The "opposites attract" relationship develops because the woman has always had a curiosity about what the other side of life is like and she plans to explore it through him.

This adventure usually turns into a nightmare because the woman winds up getting more than she expected in this situation. Run-ins with the law, domestic abuse, and constant manipulation are some of the things she may encounter during the course of this relationship. These types of issues are a direct threat to her professional and social status and she is eventually forced into terminating (if she's lucky) the relationship before things get totally out of hand and irreparable damage is done. I think that there is an old saying that goes "be careful what you wish for because you just might get it." This saying surely applies more often than not in these relationships.

I stated earlier that the woman would be lucky if she's able to leave this situation unscathed because, a lot of times, the man doesn't want to let go of a good woman, especially when he doesn't have his own life together. He will become attached to her like a parasitic leach in a codependent relationship where he has come to rely on her to supply his basic needs (food, clothing, and shelter). This type of male may be willing to do whatever is necessary to keep her in his life. That anything may include physical and mental abuse or whatever he thinks it may take to make her think that she needs him as much as he needs her. What the woman really needs to do is get a restraining order from the courts so that she may be able to move on with her life (joke).

I'm sure that some of you have seen what life can be like in the scenarios discussed above, but let's now discuss steps towards building a healthy relationship with a man that does have a firm foundation in himself and is focused on a more positive future. Ladies, when you come across a man that does have a dream or vision, it is imperative that you be as supportive as possible of his efforts to pursue his path in life. Try to learn as much as possible about his plans and make an effort to get him to include you in this process. You may be able to provide him with some assistance in areas where you may have some professional expertise. Try to be emotionally supportive because in everything that we do in life, there are going to be struggles to overcome and no man can do it all alone. He may not want to admit it initially, but he will need your help at some point and time. There's nothing like the warmth of a woman's affection to help a man make it through a rough day at work. I'll take a nice massage from a soft pair of hands anytime for stress relief (hint).

In being supportive of your man, try not to become overbearing or controlling of his vision. Otherwise, he may begin to feel that "his" dream has become "your" dream. Know when to back away and let him work independently in his own space. If you do this, he'll appreciate your understanding and ask for your assistance when it is needed. A man likes to be in control of his surroundings because he was created to be a master of his own destiny. Recognition of this critical point can decrease the chances of the two of you having unnecessary conflict and keeps his focus on the task at hand.

Finally, be sure not to set time limits on his life's plans. If he hasn't achieved a certain medium of success in a specific time frame, this doesn't necessarily mean that all of his efforts have been for naught. Continue to be a positive presence in his life and avoid making disparaging comments or criticisms about his work. He needs your support the most in this critical juncture of his life because I'm sure he'll face enough negative backlash from the outside world. Being at home with his woman should be a rest haven for a man from the madness of the world.

In short, I think you can clearly see why it is a

bad idea to get involved in a relationship with a man who lacks sound career and personal goals in his life. The relationship is never going to be a situation that is beneficial to you in any way and, in fact, it will force you to take steps backwards in your life. Man and woman were made to complement each other and not be enablers of each other's personal inadequacies. With that being said, try to choose a man that has progressive and obtainable life goals and that is willing to include you in his future plans as much as you are to include him in yours. If you do this, you will be one step closer to finding happiness in your life with the right man.

Discussion Notes

3

Social Compatibility

Now that we've discussed ways to deal with your emotional baggage before getting into a relationship and having shared professional goals with your partner, I would like to now discuss the issue of social compatibility and how it relates to the relationship process. I want to show why it is a relevant factor to have congruent personality traits with your partner for there to be an environment conducive to a healthy relationship existing between the two of you. Next, I would like to examine the importance of having some shared personal hobbies and social interests with your partner. Finally, it is my intention to explore the potential negative consequences of not having similar personality traits and shared social interests in your relationship and how they can create an atmosphere of tension and hostility that threaten the very fabric of the relationship. All in all, it is my belief that social compatibility with your mate is just as significant as having common professional aspirations to the relationship process being a fulfilling one for both parties.

Now when I think about social compatibility between a man and a woman, it brings to mind the task of putting together a jigsaw puzzle. In configuring a jigsaw puzzle, you have the task of taking several fragmented pieces of an object and putting them together in the right places in the puzzle to create the end result that is, of course, a work of art. If the pieces are not compatible with each other, you will have to try to position them elsewhere in the puzzle to find the right fit. Well, it's the same way in a relationship when you have two individuals who are trying to combine their distinctly unique personalities into a social union that is positive and beneficial for both individuals involved. If their personalities or personal interests don't match to some degree, then the chances of this social union lasting for the long haul are slim and none.

Conversely, if they do have similar likes and dislikes with respect to their personality styles and social activities, then their chances of sustaining a relationship will be significantly increased.

Ladies, when you are in the process of getting into a relationship with a man, it is critical to first do a thorough self-analysis of your personality style and how it may possibly match with his personality traits. I say this because before you get into a relationship, you should have a clear picture of who you are as a person and what needs you have that you would like to have fulfilled by your mate. By having a healthy self-identity and some clarity as to what your expectations of your man will be, you will be more likely to have your needs met and to be in a workable relationship. My thinking here is that if you are confused about who you are and what your personal needs are in a relationship, then how would you expect for a man to be able to figure out things about you that you have yet to figure out about yourself? Confusion can breed nothing but confusion and to expect it to breed anything else is insanity. That is why I feel as though this is another significant factor for any woman to consider before getting into a relationship.

To give you an example of what I mean in stating that you should find a man whose personality is in tune with yours, I would like to examine the personality styles of two different types of females. First of all, if you are a woman who is emotionally needy and likes to have a lot of personal attention from your mate, then this is a need that you have to be sure that your mate will be able to provide. You should be looking for a man that is affectionate, romantic, and into doing little things such as sending flowers to you at work to make you smile. Looking at the other end of the spectrum, if you are a woman who is a little more independent and doesn't require as much personal attention, then you should try to find a man who is of a similar mentality when it comes to relationships. The ideal type of man for this woman would be one that's secure in a situation with his mate where he doesn't have to be in her presence all the time for the relationship to be functional in his life. Being that both of you are cut from the same personality mold, then this situation should work for you. These are just two personality styles that I chose to use as examples to support my view, but you can switch these models given with your own personality style in exercising the same kind of judgment in choosing a suitable companion.

To not consider the compatible personality factor when getting into a relationship is a drastic mistake. Using the example that I gave of the woman who is emotionally needy and who craves constant affection, if she were to get involved with a man who is not the type to be affectionate with his woman, then she is just setting herself up for misery and failure. I say this because this man will never be able to satisfy one of her most basic personal needs, which is to be showered with affection. Eventually, this factor will become a problem between the two of them. When your needs are not being met in a relationship, such as the one mentioned in the example above, it will inevitably lead you to take a course of action that is not beneficial to there being harmony between the two of you.

One course of action that you may take would be to become resentful of your mate because of the lack of affection that he shows you. You may start to feel as though you are being ignored or taken for granted, and that he is being inconsiderate of your needs. In turn, he may start to get tired of your complaining that he never spends enough time with you or caters to your needs. The resentment will eventually fester inside of both of you and in some way you will begin to act out on this resentment. The "acting out" behavior will take place in the form of either verbal arguments or some type of physical confrontation. Either way, neither response is good for the relationship or for either individual.

Another course of action you may take is to find comfort in the arms of another man. Some women who feel as though their emotional needs are not being met in a relationship will find comfort in the arms of another man who may be affectionate in a way that they wish their mate would be. Yet, in still, they refuse to leave the relationship in which they are already involved. Many choose to cling to these unhappy situations because of familiarity with their partner and holding on to the faint hope that he will change over time. However, your infidelity will definitely spell disaster for the relationship because not many men can deal with, let alone forgive, a woman who cheats as opposed to a woman dealing with a man that is unfaithful. That issue is not even up for debate. Thus, this example given of the negative consequences of having incongruent personality traits with your mate should make it clear why it is not highly recommended to invest a lot of time into dating someone with whom you obviously have a drastic personality conflict.

However, if you've done a thorough personality profile of yourself and your potential mate and found some degree of compatibility, you should now think about some of the things that you like to do to have fun in your life. Make a list of some of your favorite social activities that you like to engage in during your free time. Hobbies such as bowling, roller-skating, dancing, and traveling are good examples of some fun social activities that may spark your interest. When you do meet a man that you are interested in dating, try to find out whether or not he has some of the same hobbies that you have because the two of you could participate in them together. It would be ideal to meet someone that you have everything in common with and the two of you just click on all levels, but we all know that's normally not reality. However, if you do have some of the same social interests, it gives you a healthy foundation upon which to start the relationship.

The ability to socially bond and have fun with your mate is vital to keeping the relationship progressing in a positive manner. Your mate should become your best friend over time and someone with whom you should be able to share your most special intimate moments. The best way to achieve this unique tie to your significant other is to spend time together having fun doing things that the both of you enjoy. If you have a man in your life that doesn't have some similar hobbies as you do, don't expect for the chemistry between you to last for long. I say this because if you have to find someone else to engage in fun activities with all the time other than your mate, then this will definitely leave a void in your relationship. I think most women would prefer to spend time with their man doing the things that they like to do for fun as opposed to having maybe a girlfriend or sibling serve as a stand-in.

It's not much fun being involved with someone that doesn't like to go out to the movies or dinner when these are things that you enjoy doing. This type of situation is synonymous with two ships passing in the night that occupy the same water, but are flowing in different directions. The two of you occupy some similar ground, but never seem to converge in the areas where it is most critical to have a connection for your relationship to be sustained. If this connection is not made at some time, it leaves little hope for you to be happy in this situation for the long haul. I really can't put it adequately into words why it is so important to have this social bond with your mate for your relationship to be one where there is effective, open communication. However, trust me, if it is not present, the effect will show in your relationship over time.

In evaluating your own relationships and checking to see if the social compatibility that I have mentioned above exists, be honest with yourself in assessing your situation for what it really is. If you and your mate are socially compatible, then feel secure in knowing that your relationship may be on a solid ground and more likely to last a long time. However, if there are no common personal or social traits present between the two of you, prepare yourself for a long, rough ride. The end result of these types of situations is that you wind up in a relationship that is not really a relationship, but is what I call a "sticky" social situation. What I mean by this is that neither of you is getting anything healthy out of being together, yet you both still choose to remain in this situation and deal with the drama that comes along with it.

The sad reality of this type of unhealthy relationship is something that both of you must face at some time. Just as I mentioned earlier about forcing pieces together in a jigsaw puzzle when it's obvious that they don't fit, this is exactly what the two of you are doing. Until you accept this evident fact, you will continue to remain unhappy with someone that is not able to satisfy whatever personal needs you may have. Your happiness is totally up to you so don't linger around in a relationship that was doomed to fail from the outset. Don't waste the effort trying to make the relationship something that it could never be or to make your mate be someone that it is just not in him to be. Trust me, you will wind up wasting a lot of unnecessary time when you could have met someone else who was a more "perfect" fit into your life.

Discussion Notes

4

Role Definition/Shared Responsibilities

Another problem I find that creates tension in many relationships is the inability of both partners to have clearly defined roles and responsibilities within the confines of the relationship. It appears as though, in many instances, there are no set guidelines laid out by the two, with each partners specific expectations of the other being discussed in the initial dating stage of the relationship. With no boundaries being set from the beginning of the relationship, neither individual is clear as to what would constitute "acceptable" behavior with respect to the other's individual's personal perception of how he or she should conduct himself in this social union. As a result, the emergence of conflict and arguments is highly likely to arise and to lead to a breakdown in communication between them. I believe that there should be a concerted effort made by both the man and the woman during the courtship stage of dating to discuss each other's views of what they expect of their partner within a relationship.

When you take two people who come from two distinctly, different social backgrounds, there are bound to be points of agreement as well as points of disagreement in their frames of thought. Each person will no doubt have a unique outlook on life that is shaped by his or her own personal experiences and family upbringing. For example, a man who grew up in a household where his father was the breadwinner and his mother stayed at home and raised the children is more likely to seek this same kind of intimate relationship for himself. Conversely, a woman who was raised in a household where her father was a strong, positive emotional and social presence in her life growing up is more likely to search for the same qualities that she saw in her father in her future husband.

I believe that in any relationship between two people there should be a certain level of mutual understanding with respect to each other's roles within the relationship for harmony to exist. I think that the man should have specific duties and obligations as well as the woman. That is not to say that one partner's duties and obligations are any more important than the other's, but that the two have reached agreeable terms so that neither individual violates the other's personal boundaries. The terms of agreement must be equally satisfying for both partners because if not, one of the two will feel slighted in the relationship and this will lead to a potentially negative situation.

To illustrate what I mean by having clearly established roles in an intimate relationship, let's take the example of a man and woman who have been dating for maybe five or six months. The two have been seeing each other on a regular basis and appear to enjoy spending time together. One night the woman is out on the town with her friends at a club just having a good time getting her "groove on." All of a sudden, she looks across the room and she observes the man she's been dating, but he's hugged up at the bar with another woman. Now in this situation, I ask you, is the man out of line in his behavior and does the woman have a right to be upset seeing him out with someone else in a social setting? I think that the answer to these questions is relative and based on two pertinent factors.

First of all, we have to determine whether or not the two have reached the point in this courtship where they have agreed to date each other exclusively. This agreement should not be implied, but openly shared by both parties so that there is no room for confusion. If this has been done, and both parties are in one accord on this issue, then I would say that the woman would have every right to be upset seeing him out with another woman. In addition, I think that she has a right to demand an explanation from him. I say this because if they have agreed to be in a monogamous relationship, then this may be a breach in that agreement and could bring to the surface potential fidelity issues. Without trust as a pillar in any relationship, then the relationship is not bound to last for very long.

On the flip side, if they have not openly agreed that they have become an item, then I would say that the man was not out of line to be out with another woman. If there is no commitment established, then he is a free agent and open to date anyone that he chooses to and she has no right to be upset with him. In being fair, I also say that the woman has the same right to see whomever she chooses to because the two are not locked into a binding one-on-one relationship. However, ladies, we both know that most men would have a problem if they caught you out in the public in the same situation. That's a totally different topic that may require a whole book to discuss the male ego with respect to his perceived "special" entitlements within a relationship. For now, I'll just stick to the subject at hand.

Generally speaking, when a woman gets upset in a situation like this where no committed relationship has been established, the burden of accountability lies on her and not the man. The reasoning behind this statement is that many women tend to assume that because their feelings have reached a point in the relationship where they are ready to commit to a man, then his feelings should be the same. I must emphasize two important words in my last statement and they are **assume** and **should** because these terms are conditional and suggest that no sound reasoning serves as the foundation of the woman's thinking except her projection of her own feelings onto her male counterpart. Ladies, this is a grave error that I have found that many of you make in many instances. Believe me when I tell you, speaking from a man's perspective, when a man is in love with you and is ready to seriously commit to you, you will know it. It will show in his actions and his face when he wants to claim you as his own. I'm making this point to save many of you a lot of unnecessary heartache trying to be in a relationship where you won't receive the level of commitment from a man that you may be seeking. So if you say that's he's our man, make sure that he knows this and has agreed that this is the position that he occupies in your life. Otherwise, without this clarity of his role in the relationship, you have no grounds to complain about anything that he does when he is not with you.

To give you another example of what I mean by role definition and having shared responsibilities, let's evaluate a relationship where both the man and the woman live together, work full-time, and have children. There are many issues to consider in this relationship such as how financial obligations will be divided, child-rearing expectations, and fulfillment of household maintenance responsibilities such as cooking and cleaning. There are many other issues to consider, but I have chosen to focus on just these three to expound on my view of how important it is to have defined roles and shared responsibilities within a relationship for the relationship to remain functional and satisfying for the two participants.

It is clear that both partners have a financial stake in this relationship in that they are both employed. To avoid any confusion arising over each other's financial obligations, it is imperative that the two sit down and map out a financial plan which defines who is responsible for paying what specific bills. I would suggest that they consider either splitting the bills equally (50/50) or proportionally based on income. This eliminates unnecessary confusion over finances and one less thing to have to argue about. I think we all know about the strain that financial problems can put on a relationship when one partner doesn't hold up to his end of the bargain. Trust me, it's not a pretty sight.

Secondly, I would suggest not only sharing the

responsibility of paying bills, but also to consider setting up a joint bank account. I'm not saying give up your individual bank accounts, but set up another account that you two can share for savings and investments. Both of you should set aside a set amount of money each month to save and use as part of a plan to create financial security for you and your children. Consider investing in things such as stocks and mutual funds so that your savings can collect interest and continue to grow. This will come in handy in the future when your kids have plans to go to college and when you are ready to retire.

With respect to raising children, I think that both parents should play an equally significant role in this process. Men need to grow to understand that child rearing is not a "woman's job" and take more responsibility for the upbringing of their children in areas other than providing for them financially. It is becoming increasingly obvious everyday that the old model of the mother staying at home to raise children alone is becoming obsolete and we as men need to recognize this fact. It's not feminine for a man to know how to change diapers and prepare milk bottles! Ladies, teach your mate the proper way to do these things to make the burden lighter on you. Don't let your man off the hook in thinking that it is not his responsibility to play a part in the nurturing and care of his children. He is equally obligated to aid you in these areas because he played an equal role in the procreation process, didn't he?

In addition to childcare responsibilities, both partners should share equally in the distribution of household chores. Take turns washing dishes or preparing meals so that neither of you is being overworked and begins to feel unappreciated (hint: generally the woman!). Make cleaning the house a shared activity that you two can do together or either set up a schedule where you may alternate weeks to share the responsibilities. You can look at this experience as the two of you sharing quality time together for a good cause and at the same time you are getting work done.

A final point I want to make is that even if you do reach a happy medium in your relationship with respect to sharing duties and responsibilities, always leave room for the unexpected. What I mean by this is that although your mate may have agreed to specific things in the beginning of the relationship, people are apt to change their minds on the drop of a dime. Always try to discern a person's motivation behind their actions to see if they are sincere or if they have an ulterior motive. For example, he may have no problem washing dishes and helping you cook during the courtship stage of dating, but once he gets you to let your guard down and you have fallen head over heels in love with him, he begins to flip the script. No more coming home to home cooked meals and a clean house, but instead you now come home from a hard day's work to find a kitchen full of dishes and the house in a shambles.

I believe that this change in your mate has occurred as a part of a process. First of all, his motive and intentions in agreeing to share household responsibilities with you were not done from the heart, but done to impress you and keep your interest. You see, sometimes when a man knows that he has a woman hooked, he begins to feel confident that he is now free to do whatever he wants in the relationship. He realizes that when he does kind things for his woman (i.e. sending her roses or washing her car), she will remember these things and hold on to them as pleasant memories even in the worst of times. Consequently, he no longer feels a need to impress you because he knows that he has found a special place in your heart and that no matter what he does, all will be forgiven and accepted.

Once this thinking sets in, all of the shared responsibilities in the home may be shifted onto you. It has now become your "duties" as his woman to cook and keep the house clean for him. Now you're always at home watching the kids while he is free to do whatever he chooses to do out in the streets. Ladies, if you would be honest and take a little time and analyze what I'm saying, you would have to agree that many of you have allowed yourself to be put in this situation. I advise you to stay conscious of what you want in a relationship and don't let a man smooth talk you into accepting anything less than equal treatment. If he starts off treating you a certain way, make sure he continues to treat you in the same manner. In addition, don't be afraid to walk away from the situation if he fails to improve his behavior after you have brought it to his attention.

Both of the above mentioned examples of defining different roles and having shared responsibilities for each partner clearly demonstrates how important these factors are to keeping harmony within the relationship. Of course, none of the suggestions I have made are absolute, but I gave these particular relationship scenarios to you to use as a guideline while you may be in the building or rebuilding stages of your romantic endeavors. I urge you to sit down and discuss these issues with your mate even if the two of you are not living together currently. I say this because if you do decide to take that step and move in together or get married, if you have already outlined what is expected of each other in the relationship, then that leaves more time for you to focus on other positive activities with your partner as opposed to arguing over petty issues.

Discussion Notes

5

Spending Quality Time Together

While I feel as though a relationship requires a lot of time, energy, and work from both the man and woman to make it work, I think that there should be limitations placed upon the amount of time that they spend together. This brings me to my discussion of the difference between spending quality as opposed to a specific quantity of time with your partner. It is my belief that spending too much time with someone throughout the course of a relationship can have a detrimental effect on the relationship in the long run. I believe that both the man and the woman should have a set amount of personal time away from their partner in order for harmony to remain between them. I plan to give you specific reasons to support my view of why I believe this to be true. In addition, I would like to suggest some useful time management techniques that you may be able to utilize in your relationship to make it a healthier environment for you and your mate.

Now when a man and woman first begin dating and there is some degree of chemistry between them, it's only natural that they would want to spend a lot of time with each other to become better acquainted. This is because the relationship is something new and both individuals are curious about the other person trying to find out if they may have finally found the right person to settle down with in a committed relationship. The curiosity between them is so much so that there will definitely be a lot of excitement in embarking on this adventure. During the initial period of the dating process, they may see each other four or five times a week and talk on the phone for hours every night. However, as time goes on, they may start to see each other less frequently and the phone calls will slowly decrease. What could have happened between the two of them that led to this breakdown in communication when it appeared as though things were going so well? The answer to this question is simple and I will try to spell it out at this time.

In all of our life activities, be they personal or social, that we engage in, we all should strive towards maintaining a healthy balance of time spent between these activities to insure that we don't neglect one important activity for another. Overindulgence is a universal human vice that I think we all, at some time or another, have had the task of addressing in our lives. A good example of this can be seen when we look back upon our childhood years and think about how we may have eaten too much candy when we were told not to do so by our parents. The end result, of course, was that we usually wound up getting sick. As adults, drinking too much alcohol or working too many hours on the job are two examples of doing things in excess that can have negative consequences on our mental, physical, and social wellbeing. In a relationship, if you spend too much time with your partner and neglect other aspects of your personal life, the result can be just as devastating for you as the examples listed above.

In a relationship, as I have stated before, the two persons involved must make sure that they maintain their individuality within the relationship. What I mean by this is that when some of us get into a relationship, we tend to focus all of our energy on our new partner and forget that we had a life full of activities that we engaged in before we got into a relationship. For example, you may have hung out with your girls on the weekends partying or going to the movies. However, since you've gotten into a relationship, your social interaction with your girlfriends has gradually decreased to the point that it is virtually null and void. All of your time is now devoted to spending every free moment with your new man. Over time, this will present a problem in your relationship and I would like to explain why.

When you spend an excessive amount of time with someone, I think that it has the tendency to create "burnout" in a relationship. Seeing your mate everyday, with no free time to yourself apart from him, takes away from the excitement of the gradual progression that I believe should take place between the man and woman as they strive to come into oneness with each other. When you're around him all the time, it may lead to either you or him becoming bored eventually because you've basically seen everything there is to see about each other's personalities and ways and done everything there is to do as far as social activities. This, in my view, removes the adventurous aspect of the relationship process and is a leading factor why so many relationships wind up with infidelity problems.

It is my belief that men and women have a basic need for their mate to be somewhat of a challenge to them as a part of the process of getting to know one another. It's never good to lay all of your cards on the table at one time because it doesn't leave any room for the other person to remain curious about some aspect of your personal life that he has an interest in knowing about. A certain level of mystery should always be maintained in a relationship to keep your partner's interest at its peak. Otherwise, his interest may slowly taper off and he may look elsewhere for adventure and excitement in his life. A lot of times, what we don't find at home, we have a tendency to look to external sources (I think you know what that means!) to fulfill these needs. That is why I believe that the amount of time that you spend with a man should be carefully spaced out in a calculated manner to keep him interested in remaining in the relationship with you.

Another thing ladies, just because you've meet someone that you enjoy spending time with and that you would like to have a serious relationship with, that doesn't mean that you should cut off all of your social activities that you were a part of before the relationship began. You may not want to hang out as much with your girls and that is understandable, but you should never totally eliminate this social network from your life. However, many women have a tendency to do just that. They feel as though this drastic change in their lifestyle shows their mate just how committed they are to the relationship. In their view, it sends the message that, as a woman, they are no longer into partying with their friends and that they are now ready to settle down and become a dedicated wife at some time in the near future.

While all of that sounds good in theory, in the

real world, when a man and woman spend every waking moment around each other, a lot of times it can breed not only boredom, but also tension and conflict. Many men don't like to be around their woman 24/7, and prefer to have some time to themselves apart from her. This doesn't necessarily mean that he wants to be apart from you because he has another agenda (or should I say another woman), but just that he may need room to breathe and want some individual space to himself. He may start to feel crowded by you if you want every moment of his free time to be spent with you. If you take an animal and back into a corner, it will lash out as a natural reaction. Men are no different because when a man feels crowded or pressured into something by his woman, he will have a tendency to lash out in frustration. This leaves the door open for senseless arguments to begin that could have been avoided had the two of you just taken some time apart from each other to give each other some individual space.

With that being said, I think it is clear to see that it is not the quantity of time that you spend with your mate that matters the most, but the quality of the time that you spend together. To me, quality time is any time that you spend with your significant other doing things that you both enjoy and it strengthens the bond between the two of you. It could be going to the movies, dinner, or just a quiet evening conversing as you gaze into the stars. It doesn't have to be every day, but frequent enough to develop a workable level of communication and companionship with your mate that fits into both of your personal life's schedules. This is something that I think that the two of you should be able to sit down and discuss to come up with a mutually agreed upon arrangement that will keep the relationship flowing along on a smooth course.

Going further in this discussion, just because you spend every day with your mate, that doesn't necessarily mean that the time you spent together was productive and as satisfying as the couple who chose to take time apart from each other on occasion to engage in their own separate social activities. In fact, you may wind up running out of things to do together and create a situation where the relationship is now at a standstill. The couple that sees each other less frequently is more than likely going to treasure the time that they do spend together because they've had time apart to reflect on what they mean to each other's lives. This is a luxury you are not afforded when you are constantly around your mate on a daily basis. Remember that absence does make the heart grow fonder. On the flip side, being around someone all the time can lead you to take that person for granted in not appreciating the value that they have to your life.

At this time, I would like to make a few suggestions on ways to adequately manage the time that you do spend with your mate so as to prevent boredom and complacency from becoming factors within your relationship. First of all, when you initially start dating a man, try seeing him maybe once or twice a week and call him maybe once a day, but no more than that. That way you keep the excitement and anticipation of seeing him again alive in your mind and heart. In addition, if he is really interested in you, he will be just as anxious and full of anticipation to see you again. Next, make sure that you don't put excessive pressure on him to rearrange his personal schedule to fit you into his plans. For example, he may have Friday nights set aside for him and his male friends to hang out on the town and you decide to ask him to change his plans to spend those evenings with you now that the two of you have become an item. I think that this is an unfair request for you to make because as long as he is not engaging in activities that are a threat to the relationship (i.e cheating), then a man is entitled to have some quality time for himself to socially network with his friends. On the same note, I think that you should have set days of your own for you to have some quality time apart from him to do some things that you enjoy doing with your friends or family members.

By taking this time apart from each other to have fun, it gives the two of you something to talk about when you do see each other again. You can look at this with the idea in mind that the days you do spend together are an opportunity for you both to laugh and converse about each other's individual exploits from the days that you don't see each other. This will definitely keep the doors of communication open between the two of you and lead to a stronger friendship developing within the confines of your relationship. We have already discussed why having a friendship with your mate is important to the relationship process and this is just another means to strengthen that bond.

Thus, I think that I have painted a clear picture as to why it is more important to spend quality time with your mate as opposed to spending an exorbitant quantity of time together. In a relationship, a man and woman should grow together at a slow, steady pace as opposed to rushing to get to know everything about each other all at once in a short period of time. Spending time apart to do some things with others besides your mate will afford you an opportunity to maintain your individual freedom within the relationship and, at the same time, reduce the chances of unnecessary tension developing between the two of you because of relationship 'burnout". Having patience and effective time management skills are a must to maintain a healthy balance in your life between your intimate relationship and the other areas of your personal life.

Discussion Notes

6

Keep the Flames Burning

Now this chapter may get a little steamy for those of you with sensitive ears when it comes to issues relating to sexuality and romance. You may want to get a cold glass of water to cool you down while you're reading this (smile). In this portion of the book I want to explore the idea that a lively sexual connection must be maintained within a relationship for it to be an adventure that will continually be enjoyed by both partners. I want to make a clear distinction between sex and romance because I don't think that many of us are able to distinguish between the two entities. I plan to discuss why having a healthy sex life is a crucial factor in a relationship and how it can lead to better communication between the two individuals involved. Finally, I want to make a few suggestions about ways to spice up those intimate moments with that special person so that you can keep his interest for the long haul as well as increase the level of pleasure that you may experience during intimacy.

First of all, when I think about sex between a man and woman, I see it as the ultimate joining of two separate parts of one universal whole coming together to form the perfect union. I don't think that there is a stronger bond that can be shared between the sexes than the act of making love. Sex is a natural thing and should be an act that is mutually enjoyable for both participating actors. However, I don't think that we are born knowing how to be a good lover to our mates, but that we have to develop these skills over time and through much practice. That is not to say that I am suggesting that we all go out and just sleep around to enhance our love making techniques, but I do believe that every sexual experience should be a part of our learning process as we strive to become better lovers to our significant others.

When a man and woman first meet each other, it is the physical attraction that exists between them that generates curiosity and makes them want to find out more about each other. Many women may deny this and say that this is a shallow point of view, but I say to you, let's be real. It's not just men who look at the physical first, but women also do the same thing except they use a little more discretion and are more tactful in their approach (smile). Realistically, if this is your first encounter with a man, what else do you have to go on besides finding what you see before your eyes as appealing? Now we all have to be honest and agree that none of us want to wake up every morning next to someone that we see as having an unpleasant looking face to view. I think you know what I mean in stating this mildly (laugh).

I'm not saying that he has to be some muscular man who's extremely handsome to catch your attention, but I am saying that it is something about his physical appearance that intrigued you enough to give him the time of day and for you to consider the possibility of dating him. It might be the way he walks, the way he smells, or just his aura that makes you want to see what this man is all about. Either way, any of these things tend to spark that initial physical attraction that may lead to the developing of a sexual relationship between the two of you. This is a fact that neither a man or a woman can be honest about with self and deny.

Although I've mentioned things such as having similar life goals and shared responsibilities as being vital to a good relationship, I can't underscore how important it is to have a good sex life with your partner in order to keep his interest. Not only is it important in keeping his interest, but good sex in a relationship eases tension between the man and woman and makes it easier for them to interact in a friendly manner. When both you and your mate connect on all of the other areas of the relationship and the sex is good, there is little room for unnecessary tension to exist between the two of you. Sex is a tool that can be used not only for procreation, but also for pleasure and stress relief. Thus, for these reasons, I think that both the man and woman must contribute as much of themselves as possible to keeping the sexual chemistry alive in a relationship for it to be long lasting.

If during the course of a relationship you start to not pay as much attention to your man's physical needs, his eyes may begin to wander and look elsewhere. For example, let's just say that you may not want to have sex as much as he does or you are not open to trying something new in your sexual activities. It's these types of issues that can affect your relationship in a very negative way if there is no justifiable reason for your lack of interest in sex (i.e. health or mental issues). I'm not saying this in any way to justify the actions of a man who cheats because a man is going to do what he has in his heart to do regardless. I'm merely suggesting that if the relationship started with a lot of sexual sparks jumping off between the two of you and gradually your desire for sex starts to taper off, you may wish to ask yourself whether or not you may have played a part in his straying from the relationship. Your lack of interest in sex may lead him to become bored and to look for excitement in the arms of another woman.

Many women tend to want to look at the other woman as being the villain in ruining their relationship and not look at how their not being on their job in the bedroom may have contributed to his wandering eye. It is hard for any of us to admit to our faults especially if we may have been influential in someone else's wrongdoing. Human pride is a quality that usually blinds our ability to see how our actions may have had a strong enough impact on someone else to influence their decision making in a negative way. Don't blame another woman for doing something for your man that you have the power to do and choose not to do for whatever reason. The ball is in your court to correct the situation if you see the relationship as having enough value to your life.

Now I know many women personally who, after they have been in a relationship for a while, tend to ration out the sex to their man when they feel as though he may deserve some (laugh). You see, I think a lot of women recognize the power that sex has traditionally had over many men and they use this to their advantage. However, today, this type of behavior doesn't have as much effect on a man as it used to in the past. Even the average man today recognizes that he has an abundance of beautiful, professional minded women to choose from that are single and willing to satisfy any sexual desires that he may have without inhibitions. With that being said, a man has no logical reason to put up with a woman that doesn't want to fulfill his sexual needs because he can easily replace her with someone else who is submissive to his desires. Think about this seriously because I believe that many of you have been and will be confronted with this dilemma if you are a female who plays these types of sexual rationing games. Many of you have lulled yourselves into a false sense of security thinking that a man will settle for this type of sexual game for the long haul. You better wake up and see what's real!

Getting into a routine of doing the same thing over and over again becomes monotonous after awhile for anybody in any type of activity in life. This could be true with work, going to the same social circles, or even just wearing your hair in the same style (now I know you can feel me on this point!). We all have a tendency to search for an outlet that may add some adventure or adrenaline rush to our boring lives. Sex in a relationship is no different and should be looked at as being just as vital as all of our other life activities. That is why it is important to change things up every now and then to make life more fun.

I think that if you love your man and have decided within yourself that he is the one that you want to be with in an intimate relationship, you should be open to doing almost anything to make him happy. That is, of course, as long as what he wants does not cause harm to you in any way, be it physically or mentally. If you know that your man is the type who likes to have sex four or five times a week or several times a day and your sexual desire for him is not the same, then maybe the two of you are not sexually compatible. Going further, if the two of you are not on the same wavelength sexually, and since sex is an integral part of an intimate relationship, I think that it may be time for you to reassess your relationship to see if it should continue.

I have said it many times thus far that good communication is a must to have in your relationship. Sexual chemistry between partners is one of those mediums of communication that needs to be maintained and constantly improved upon if the relationship is to last. As a man, I know that after coming home from a hard day's work there is no greater joy than to come home to a beautiful woman that is willing to do whatever is needed to help me relieve my stress sexually. It doesn't have to be every night, but frequent enough to keep me satisfied. For me, this is a must in a relationship and I would never be in a relationship with a woman who could not satisfy me intimately. I know some of you may say that this is kind of blunt, but I believe in being real. If your partner is not into the same things that you are sexually, even though he may care for you as a person, eventually he is going to stray, more often than not, and find someone else to take care of his physical cravings.

In arguing that a woman should be willing to fulfill her man's sexual needs, that leads me to assume that her sexual attraction for her man is the same as it was in the beginning. If the physical attraction has faded away, and she's not willing to do anything to bring it back, then it's safe to say that this relationship won't last much longer. However, if you are in a relationship where the sex has become boring between you and your partner and you want to make a sincere effort to bring the sparks back, I would like to make a few suggestions to you to try to rekindle the flames of romance. At this time, I want to discuss some romantic things that you can do to possibly keep his interest by spicing things up in your bedroom. I want to discuss the difference between sex and romance and how you can use both tools to keep your man at home and not in the streets with another woman. Finally, I also want to propose ways that you can inspire him to want to do more to please you sexually in giving your body the attention that it may need.

First of all, there is a significant difference between having sex and being romantic. Just because you have sexual intercourse with someone doesn't mean that it was a romantic interlude. Sex, at times, can be non-emotional and very impersonal if there is no special connection between the participants. Romance, on the other hand, comes into play when there are emotional ties between the two individuals in the relationship. It's the non-sexual foreplay that leads up to an evening of intense lovemaking. It can include things such as sending flowers, cards or erotic gifts (use your imagination) to your partner to peak their sexual curiosity. I submit to you ladies that not every man knows how to be romantic with a woman and that some of you may have never had any experience romancing a man. If you haven't had any experience at this, let me now take the time to give you a few pointers.

In romancing a man, one of the first things you should always try to do is be spontaneous and unpredictable in your actions. No man wants a woman who is not open to new sexual experiences or willing to try new things. If you are the type of woman that is reserved and shy about her sexuality, try doing something out of your character to catch his attention. You have to always keep your man on his toes and conscious of the fact that he has a beautiful woman in his life. If you don't, he may begin to take you for granted. It's your job to remind him of your value and why he chose you to be his woman.

Now let me give you an idea of how to set up a romantic evening that's sure to please your man. When he comes over to see you one night, have the house clean with the candles lit up in every room and a nice, sweet smelling fragrance burning in the air. One of my favorite scents is a body oil called "Lick me all over" (seriously, I didn't make up the name, but it fits!) that can be burned in an oil burner to produce a scent that is sure to set the mood right. Once the atmosphere in your home is set up to your liking, relax yourself in a nice bubble bath to ease your mind. If your mind is at ease from the trials of your day at work, then you'll have less time to think about other things and can dedicate the rest of your evening to pleasing your man.

Next, after you step out of tub, make sure you put on a nice and sweet smelling perfume or body lotion because nothing catches a man's eye more than a woman that smells good enough to eat (smile). Something from Bath and Body Works (Cotton Blossom or maybe Sweetpea) or Victoria's Secret (Pear) should do the trick. A perfume that is one of my personal favorites to smell on a woman is called "212" by Caroline Herrera. Now that you have yourself smelling sweet with a scent that you know he would like to smell on you, slip into a sexy piece of lingerie that accents all of your best physical features. When picking something out, think about something that you know will make it hard for him to take his eyes off of you for the rest of the evening once he see you in it. Make it something so appealing that he'll be anxious to get you out of it as soon as possible. It's got to be something sensuous and tasteful, not trashy (unless, of course, you and your man like it that way!).

Now that you have the house set up displaying a nice and cozy type of scenery and, of course, you're looking lovely as ever, the time is now right for you to set your plan in motion. When he walks in the door, greet him with a warm hug and a light kiss just to wet his appetite, but don't give him too much at one time. Take him by the hand and lead him to the couch or the room of your choice because remember, you're in charge. Once you're in the room of your choice, the time is now right for you to utilize the skills that you have in your bag of tricks to entice, tease, romance, and satisfy your man for the rest of the night. Use the entire house as your playground to explore new erotic adventures with your mate that you may have never done before or that you have not done in a while.

Start him off with a nice massage from head to toe using some kind of warming massage oil. Make sure you do a good enough job to inspire him to want to reciprocate the favor and give you a massage that is just as stimulating. After the massage is done, a heavy dose of foreplay is strongly recommended. Items such as strawberries, melted chocolate, honey, and whipped cream are some of my favorite tools to use, but I would rather not say how or where they are utilized (smile). I didn't want to get too graphic because I like to leave some things up to the imagination. So in that case, use your best judgment in fulfilling your sexual fantasies with your man. If you do these things and they don't create any renewed or heightened sexual interest between you and your man, then maybe it's just not meant to be for the two of you. However, if after you try an evening like this with your man and your sex life gets off the hook from that point on, all I ask is that you just send me an e-mail to tell me "Thank you" (joke).

This is just one example of a romantic evening that you can plan to share with your man, but I'm sure that if you put your creative juices to work you can come up with some other sexually exciting scenarios that will spark your man's interest. If you've been with a man for a while, you should know what his sexual likes and dislikes are because you must have been doing something right in the beginning to make him come back for more. With that being said, continue to do those things that you know he likes and he will have less of a reason to be out in the streets looking for pleasure from another woman. Just like at work, if you don't perform up to the job duties required, you may be fired and replaced. Keep this in mind and make sure that your "work" performance stays up to par so that you can stay "employed" because the same principle holds true in relationships.

In stating that you must be willing to do whatever is necessary to keep your man sexually satisfied, I'm not saying that to let him off the hook in satisfying your needs. He has an equal responsibility to satisfy your needs as well and you have the job of making sure that he lives up to your expectations in the bedroom. However, the only way a man is going to know what things satisfy you sexually is for you to be open enough verbally in communicating this to him from the start. A man and woman in a relationship should have an open door of communication between them so that they are able to spell out clearly what they want from each other. If this open door of communication is not present, then that is not only going to lead to a host of problems in the bedroom, but in other areas of the relationship as well.

I've heard many women talk about how they've faked orgasms from time to time in relationships just to stroke their man's ego so he doesn't feel inadequate sexually. I personally feel as though this is one of the most ridiculous things that you can do in a relationship for several reasons. First of all, if he thinks that he's pleasing you and he really isn't, then you're being dishonest with him and have no one to blame for your lack of sexual pleasure but yourself. Once you're dishonest with someone in a relationship and then try to come back later to undo your lie, that person is justified in not trusting what you say out of your mouth because of your actions. Going further, your dishonesty will truly make him feel inadequate with you sexually once he finds out and he may become more selfish in just trying to quench his own sexual appetite, while paying even less attention to your needs. This will definitely begin to have you feeling sexually frustrated (sorry ladies you all are no different than men in some areas). On top of that, you're wasting your own time taking your clothes off and getting undressed to lay down with a man and getting no personal enjoyment out of it. That makes no sense at all. You might as well stay fully clothed and just have verbal communication for all that's worth. You can only play with sex toys and use methods of self-stimulation for so long before you want the real thing in your bed with you (smile).

With that being said ladies, don't be afraid to tell your man if he's doing something wrong during the act of making love. However, I suggest doing so in a tasteful manner. For example, if he is performing oral sex on you and he may not be doing a good job in getting you excited, playfully guide him to your erogenous zones so that you can get the most out of the sexual experience. Going further, if during the act of making love he may be going too fast for you, tell him to slow down in a nice sensuous tone so that it doesn't disrupt the flow. You've got to be willing to be verbal in expressing your sexual desires and needs to your man if you expect for him to please you. Otherwise, the both of you are just wasting each other's time. Trust me, a man loves it when a woman gives instructions during sex, but does so in an enticing manner. Utilize your skills the best way you know how to keep your man satisfied sexually and I guarantee you that if he's feeling you the same way that you're feeling him, he'll return the favor.

Discussion Notes

7

Game Recognize Game

I'm sure that many of you have seen the movies "Love Jones" and "Two Can Play That Game." These two movies, in my view, depict the reality of many relationships that exist among our generation today. They showcase all of the mind games and manipulative behavioral patterns that are prevalent among both males and females and how they tend to sidetrack the relationship from being a mutually enjoyable situation for both individuals. Also highlighted is the idea that a relationship will always be a power struggle between the man and woman to see who has the upper hand in the relationship.

This, to me, fosters the notion that a man and woman can't have a balance of power in a relationship. That notion is absurd, but is one that is embedded in the psyche of many of us and needs to be explored further to see the insanity in this way of thinking.

In both movies, you have two couples comprised of professional minded young, Black men and women who can't seem to get things right to make their relationship work. In "Love Jones", the main characters, Darius and Nina, played by Larenz Tate and Nia Long, are two young people who are evidently both scared of commitment, yet somehow manage to fall for each other unexpectedly. Both individuals are set in their ways and seem unwilling to compromise with the other for the sake of making the relationship work. As a result, there are many trust issues, unresolved past relationships, and professional aspirations of both individuals that seem to get in the way of their being together. The movie winds up being a series of makeup's and breakup's before they finally accept the reality that they were meant to be together. They were so set in their ways that they almost let a good opportunity for a loving relationship to exist slip through their hands because of their egos.

In "Two Can Play that Game", the scenario is a little bit different. Vivica Fox and Morris Chestnut, who play the two main characters, Shante and Keith, are involved in a heated relationship that appears to be going along smoothly until one fateful evening. On that night, Keith cancels a date with Shante and tells her that he has to work late. However, while Shante is out with her girls that same night, she sees him in the club with another woman (remember the scenario discussed in chapter 4?). This one event sets Shante off on a mission to teach Keith a lesson that he will never forget. She has developed a 10-day plan to get her man "in line" and make him "behave" like she wants him to. This winds up being a sad mistake that almost winds up costing her a good man. I say this because instead of her asking him for an explanation as to why he was out with another woman, she just jumped to her own conclusion and plotted her next course of action. I don't think that he had deceitful intentions with the other woman, but I do agree that he may have been out of line to be caught in such an uncompromising situation.

Shante, to me, had control issues that she needed to address. When a man or woman wants to be a domineering presence in a relationship, it tends to put the other individual on the defensive and can lead to drama and conflict between them. Trying to impose your will on your partner to suit your own personal needs can only lead to a heated situation developing at some point and time. I think that many of you have these similar control issues in relationships that hamper your ability to maintain a relationship. As a result, many of you play these same kind of mind games that Shante played in the movie to get your man to do something that you want him to do, even if it is something that is beneficial to the relationship. However, what winds up happening is that he starts to play the same mind games that you play and the both of you lose focus on the relationship. What you have at this point is a big mess that you may not be able to clean up if the games get too far out of hand. This is exactly what almost happened in the movie and does happen quite often in real life relationships today.

In my dealings with women in my personal relationships, I have tried to hold fast to the idea that honesty and forthrightness are the best means of approaching the situation, be it a committed or casual relationship. In being honest with someone from the start with respect to what kind of relationship I would like to have with them, I try to eliminate the possibility of a woman misconstruing my motives and actions. If I am interested in getting to know a woman to see if we may be able to possibly develop a serious relationship, I have no problem saying just that directly to her. Conversely, if I am only interested in a casual, intimate relationship with a young lady, I have no difficulty in being blunt in saying that is what I want also.

By handling things this way, I leave it up to the woman to decide if she wants to pursue the situation any further. This approach should reduce the potential for drama and saves a lot of time for both of us in that no woman can say that she was deceived or manipulated by my ill intentions. However, we all know that there are some of us who tend to interpret reality as we choose to and tend to take what others do in their actions and rationalize them from our own warped perspective. We call those individuals "stalkers" and leave it up to the legal system to handle (smile).

Now I've heard quite a few women say in conversation that a man deceived them into thinking that he wanted a serious, committed relationship when all he really wanted was casual sex. Even more talk about how they can't believe that their man may have cheated on them with another woman because he appeared to be so committed to the relationship. An even larger group of women are willing to forgive their man if he cheats on them because they rationalize it in their heads that he won't do it again. All of these ways of thinking leave you susceptible to being hoodwinked time and time again by a man if you don't open up your eyes to see the reality of your situation.

I can agree that many of us men do have a way of being surreptitious in our actions with women to get what we want. However, ladies, I think you give men way too much credit. What I mean is that a man usually sends you a lot of warning signs unconsciously in his actions that tell you that he's not sincere in stating his agenda for you. The problem is that many of you choose not to see the truth even when it is staring you smack dead in your face. The sad reality that I find is that when some women are in love, they will do anything and say anything to hold on to their man just to have a man.

Some women will rationalize their man's cheating behavior in arguing that the love between them is strong enough to withstand his infidelity or that they may have done something wrong to warrant him cheating on them. Some will go so far as to cheat on him as a way to get back at him for his behavior and think that this will make the relationship go back to being normal. To me, all of this madness in your thinking and the actions you take in accord with this thinking show why a relationship can sometimes be an unhealthy thing to have in your life. The question that I ask you is that will you allow these time consuming mind games to continue to be a part of your life or will you make a concerted effort to remove this nonsense from your life to find a real relationship that is built on a solid foundation? Think about that question.

To support my contention that a man generally shows you in his actions what he really feels about you and if he's really interested in a serious relationship, I would like to give you a few examples. If a man is always in the club with his friends every night of the weekend, it's safe to say that he's not really interested in a committed relationship. A man that is serious about being in a monogamous situation is not going to be in an environment that is basically for single individuals looking for a mate unless he's on the hunt for something, or should I say someone, for himself. However, some of you actually believe that your man hangs out in the club and is not fooling around with other women. That's like putting a child in a candy factory and expecting him not to sample the merchandise. It's not that much hanging with the fellas in the world with no females involved and you can trust me on that.

Secondly, if a man tells you that he loves you, but is afraid to commit to a monogamous relationship after you've been together for a while (at least a year), please believe that most of the time, you're not the only female in his life. You may be the one that he cares about the most, but he still has at least one other female on the side when he wants to break up the monotony of being with you. I say this because if a man has been involved with you in a relationship for a protracted period of time, he basically knows your strengths and weaknesses as a person and he knows whether or not he wants you to be the one that he settles down with for the long haul. Don't believe him when he says that he's confused because it's just a ploy on a man's part to have his cake and eat it too. You have to ask yourself whether or not your time is more valuable than to accept being in this type of relationship.

A third illustration I want to give you is that of the man who tells you that he loves you, but basically does nothing for you either mentally or financially. I didn't mention sexually because he will make an effort to satisfy your sexual needs. The reasoning here is that he believes that this is one of your weaknesses and an easy avenue for him to take to get what he wants from you (money, clothes, etc). As I said before, women tend to place a stronger emotional attachment to sex than men do. Ladies, I'm sure that many of you have had that one man who made you so weak in the knees with some good loving that you turned the bank book over to him and told him that whatever is yours is also his (laugh). I know it's true because I've done it a few times myself to a few of you in the past. It's not something that I'm proud of, but I'm just keeping it real.

The problem in this situation is that the "good" feeling that this man may give you sexually has blinded your ability to reason with reality. You are not able to see that he is just using you for all that he can get from you and that he doesn't really want you as a person. Once he has drained all of your resources, he'll be out of your life quickly. In turn, you're left behind brokenhearted with no man and mad bills to pay. Stop me right here, if I'm telling you a lie (laugh).

I think that the reason some of you wind up in some of the above mentioned situations has to do with internal self-esteem issues you may have for whatever reason. I say this because if your love of self were at a level where you fully appreciated your value as a human being, you would not allow someone to manipulate you and treat you in such a degrading manner. Your recognition of your self-worth would not let you allow any man to use you or mistreat your emotions. You would be able to see the difference between love and lust and not make up a distorted perception of reality to remain in the types of relationships that I have described above. Finally, your longing for love and a soulmate would not blind your rational thinking and thought process to the point that you accept treatment less than that of a queen.

A man who is serious about having a committed relationship wants to see the same self-confidence that he possesses displayed in his woman. He wants a woman that is quick to pull his card if he even thinks about stepping out to be with another woman. In addition, he has to believe that she will be strong enough to leave him if he ever cheated on her. If you have a man thinking that way and he really is in love with you, trust me, he truly values you in his life and he wouldn't think about messing that up for a meaningless fling. If a man doesn't value you to this degree, then you shouldn't have him in your life.

In summing up, the mental games that are played in today's relationships will never work out to create a situation that is beneficial to your life. That is why I suggest that you do your part to try and eliminate any man from your life that comes to you with games in mind. If you don't, the relationship will only hamper your growth and become a major waste of time. Make sure a man respects you and appreciates your unique value as a woman. Make sure that he shows you sincerely in his actions how he feels about you and not just with empty words. No relationship is worth you losing your self-respect over or you becoming that "Bag Lady" mentioned in the first chapter. If you have to manipulate a man for him to be in your life, then you don't need him. Tricks and games are for kids so if you've decided that you are a mature adult, then make a conscious effort to put the games aside and I assure you that your future relationships will be much more prosperous.

Discussion Notes

8

What Does It All Mean?

As I stated in the introduction, ***For My Sisters*** is my attempt to try to stimulate intelligent discussion between young men and women in their 20's and 30's about relationship issues that we confront on a daily basis. I hope that after reading this book women are inspired to do a honest self-evaluation of their approach to relationships currently to see if any of the factors that I have mentioned in the text may have some validity in assessing their shortcomings in their attempts to find that one fulfilling love relationship in their lives. The 7 key areas that I have presented in this book should serve as a blueprint of sorts for you to utilize to get your relationship endeavors started on the right track or to improve the status of your current relationship. It is my sincerest hope that I have done a thorough job in achieving the objectives that I set out to accomplish with this work. I plan to judge my level of success upon the responses that I receive from you in your comments and criticisms of this book.

One of the primary points that I have tried to drive home in each of the chapters is that you must maintain a healthy self-identity throughout the course of any your intimate relationships. If not, you leave yourself open to being disrespected and taken for granted by someone who is not able to appreciate your special value as a woman. In this society, it appears as though there is a certain amount of social pressure on women to find a suitable mate by a certain age. This widespread frame of thought has led many of you to have self-esteem issues in feeling as though you have to have a man to be complete as a woman. As a result, I believe that many of you settle for getting involved with the first man who comes along who appears to be a good candidate to be Mr. Right. However, this man, more often than not, winds up not being the right one for you, but you still choose to remain with him just to say that you have someone in your life. This is a way of thinking that you must address if you ever expect to find true happiness in your life.

While I understand that it is a natural human

feeling to not want to be alone in our lives, this does not justify getting involved in a relationship just for the sake of being in a relationship. You must understand that your happiness in life should never be contingent upon someone else's perception of what should make you happy. Instead, it should be based upon your own personal viewpoint of what you feel internally can bring you joy and contentment in your life. You can only reach this point in your evolution as an individual when you accept the reality that you must become comfortable with yourself first before you can expect to find a relationship with another person on an intimate level that is healthy to have in your life. In other words, being love in with a man should complement the love that you feel for yourself and serve to aid you in your growth as a human being as opposed to being a hindrance to your life's plans. Get to know you first and foremost before you even think about starting a relationship. This one factor alone can save you a lot of time and unnecessary heartache.

A second theme that was discussed throughout the book is that you must be able to communicate effectively with your partner on all levels to sustain a relationship. Communicating effectively does not mean having endless, dramatic arguments with your mate, but that you must be able to talk to one another in a calm, rational manner. As I stated earlier, I would like to put an end to the drama that we experience in our relationships and we have to be able to talk to each other sensibly if we expect to achieve this objective. I don't know about you, but I'm sick of hearing about so many relationships that have ended on a sour note because the two individuals involved didn't take the time to express themselves maturely to each other to possibly resolve their relationship issues. A lot of potentially good relationships have eroded because of this factor and I hope that I have given you enough reasons in my writing for you to find more effective ways to communicate with your significant other than you may have done in the past. It is my belief that if two people can't sit down and talk to each other peacefully to resolve their differences, then they shouldn't be together.

A third and final theme that I have tried to stress is that there are some good men out there to be found, but that you must be more selective in your choices if you expect to find the right one for you personally. I understand that we all will make mistakes in our choices in life, but I tend to think that you can reduce your margin of error in choosing the right man by exercising better decision making in your thought process. For example, you should know that if a man has no job or plans to find a job, there is nothing that he can do for you in your life that is beneficial to you. You need to be real with yourself about this fact. Don't be sidetracked because he is nice looking or has a charismatic personality because that's just a smokescreen that your lower self (smile) creates to lead you to make poor choices in life. When you let superficial factors blind you to evident truths in life, you have no one to blame for your misfortune but yourself. You must accept responsibility for your actions and make a sincere effort to change them if you expect to have better results in the future. I know that there are a lot of good men that you may have overlooked chasing after the ones that you knew in your subconscious mind were bad for you. Try giving one of those "nice" guys a chance and see how it turns out. You may be in for a pleasant surprise in more ways than you could ever imagine.

In conclusion, I hope that this book was as much of an adventure and learning experience for you as it was for me to write. It took a lot of hard work and intense thought for me to compose, but every hour spent was well worth it if my work touches the life of just one woman out there who is struggling to find her "soulmate". This alone would make my labor something that I am proud of and make me feel as though I have contributed something noteworthy to possibly aiding one of my female counterparts in finding happiness in her life. I don't pretend to have all of the solutions to all of the relationship problems that we confront as a generation, but it is my sincerest hope that I have opened the door to enlightening the female mind as to how a man looks at the female's role in the relationship process.

Bonus Section -

Poetry Selections

Writing poetry has always been one of my favorite hobbies since I was child. It's something about the sound of words when they are combined together in a rhythmic fashion that has always caught my attention. I like the way that a poet is able to tell a lengthy story or deliver an in depth life lesson in such a clever way by using the least amount of words. To me, poetry is a universal language that we all can relate to in some way or form. I think that we all have, at some time or another, sat down in our own private moments, either as a child or an adult, and composed a poem to express some feeling or thought that has been confined within the recesses of our subconscious mind. It may have been to express our love for another person or to convey a profound thought about some troubling life experience. Either way, poetry is a literary art form that I believe enables the writer to be free to speak on any subject that he chooses to without expecting harsh criticism from others. With that being said, it is only fitting that I ended this book with a small collection of relationship oriented poetry for you to enjoy.

In reading through the poetry pieces that I have chosen to include in this book, I want you to think about the underlying message that is conveyed in each piece to see if it may relate to some life experience that you may have encountered in your personal intimate relationships. I have attempted to cover every aspect imaginable of relationship issues or situations to give you a well-rounded selection of poems to read. I've discussed everything from finding true love to falling out of love or even being in love with someone else when you are already in a relationship. In addition, I've also tried to express my respect and admiration for women and the special attributes that they have which they are able to contribute to the relationship process. Some of the pieces you may find to be a little on the erotic side, but I think that you are mature enough to handle the content (smile). Thus, I hope that you enjoy my poetry and find it stimulating to your thoughts in a positive manner. I have made an effort to give you firsthand insight into some of my own personal relationship experiences and preferences to show you that some of us men also have a sensitive side to us.

What's In A Woman

Sincerity and compassion
you possess a love that's unrivaled
far beyond the realm of human comprehension.
God made no mistake in making you
for you are the embodiment of his love for man.

You've sacrificed of yourself for others
with little or no regard
for your own well being.
It was you who brought us through slavery
and raised all these bad ass kids alone.

Your beauty is much more than meets the eye
but my third eye sees far beyond
what you visibly show.
You've been so patient and understanding of us men
praying for us, waiting anxiously
hoping one day that we would grow.

That we would evolve to be the kind of men
to appreciate and not abuse you
for your abuse is our self-destruction.
A nation can rise no higher than its women
a wise man gave me this infinite lesson.

To this end, I share these thoughts with you
as a small token of the love that I have in my heart.
In recognition of all the ingredients
that make up you as a woman
it just shows that God wisely molded and crafted you
to be the essence of perfection.

When Love Is Right

Don't be afraid to say what U feel
because love always leaves room for us to fail
If what U feel inside is truly real
in the end, eternal happiness will always prevail

Love that's shared is inevitable
destined to come into fruition
The presence of another to intervene
never worry, because there's no competition

What is meant to be will be
given time, all the answers will unfold
Be prepared to receive what's rightfully yours
because that which is divine is out of our control

It's kinda like when the planets are aligned
or when the brightness of the stars
illuminates the sky
When Love Is Right, it's just right
you won't have to ask why

Just be open to new revelations
kinda like a virgin exposed for the very first time
When Love Is Right, it's just right
so relax and let it ease your mind

When I See U, I See Me

When I see your smile
U make me blush.
Your warmth captivates
every inch of the man inside of me.

Every time I think of **U**, I think Of **Us**
it's like we've melted into liquid form
and become one.
In my intimate thoughts, I think to myself
would it be too much to ask for U to give me a son?

For U to raise him with your love
and every gentle caress of your hands
All I've seen is the rough side of life
but daily, for U, I'm striving to be a better man

I now see a new beginning
as though my life has taken a turn for the better
There's no mountain too high to climb
as long as we're together

The resemblance we've developed is evident
everytime that I look into your eyes
If I ever awoke without U beside me
inside, I think my soul would die

Revolutionary Love

I'm listening to what you say
because your words convey a message of love.
They're telling me that
you're yearning for affection
that only a man can give if his heart is sincere.

That's why I come to you with open arms
and no inhibitions whatsoever.
I'm just a conscious man, humbled by reality
who possesses an understanding ear.

Ears that are able to hear
all of your inner thoughts and insecurities.
Those thoughts that you held
deep within your soul, protected
at least until I came into your life.

What was so difficult for so many to see
yet alone understand in its entirety.
That all you really wanted was a man
one who was complete
and able to treat you right.

To be your lover and best friend
because it's the friendship
that cements the foundation.
Knowledge and wisdom combined
equals man and woman
manifesting a love that can raise
the consciousness of a nation.

Like A Summer Breeze

I watch the wind blow through your hair
as I stare, astounded, better yet in awe
Right before my eyes, a living witness
the most beautiful woman I ever saw

I'm trying to play it cool
stay collected and calm
But the anxiety is building
nervous, sweat fills my palms

I asked U your name
U told me, in a delicate, angelic voice, so heavenly
I just have one question
could U be the one to fulfill my destiny?

That mystery woman
elusive, the one that I wanna hold sacred
I'm prepared to give U a lifetime of love
that's if U wanna take it

Intellectual Sex Appeal

From A Secret Admirer

Your mind entices me
I'm curious to know more
U intrigue me to conversate
and take the time to explore

Dignified in your walk
I see U like to read
To take me to the next level
that's the type of woman that I need

One who appreciates her sexuality
without exposing her flesh
A brother gotta come correct
she won't settle for less

A lady in every aspect
her mental supports the physical frame
Staring from a distance
I just wanna know your name

In The Name of Love

I played my best hand
put in much work
But now it's time to accept reality
and look past the hurt

No need to beat a dead horse
for love has blown away like the wind
A road slowly traveled
picking up the pieces, where do I begin?

These wars of the heart can shatter
leave the soul fully exposed
To begin a new chapter in this saga
some doors must be closed

But if it's all for the better
tell me, who are we to judge?
Many lives are filled with regrets
in the name of this thing called **Love**

The Taste of Forbidden Fruit

How could I be so deeply in love with you
when I know your heart's not in the right place?
I guess that's my dilemma
that I have to answer for my damn self.

You tell me that you feel the same way
but every time that I ask you to stay for the night
you never seem to comply with my wishes.
Instead you return home to a man
that ain't even got you in his faintest thoughts.

He never listens to your cries for attention
instead he compounds your pain
with nothing but more lies.
He tells you the things that you want to hear
while I try to tell you all the things
that your soul yearns to receive.

Addictive love is insanity for the both of us
yet I can't seem to break free from your grip.
While you, in turn, cling to me for affection
because you know I'll always be there
for you in your time of need.

Man, this is driving me crazy
that I could let myself fall in love
with another man's woman.
Now I understand God's infinite wisdom
and why he told Adam not to eat that damn fruit.

Can We Talk

All this arguing, screaming, fighting and fussin'
I just can't seem to understand
Why we can't sit down
and have a peaceful discussion

So much tension in the air
yet we both claim that we care
I can't tell by the way we act
I'm about to lose my mind up in here

Have things gotten so bad
that we have to call each other names
We're both supposed to be adults
too old for such childish games

Can We Talk for a minute
and try to put an end to this
You're not my enemy and I'm not yours
so all of this is senseless

Without communication all we have
is insanity, confusion, and so much frustration
It's gotta be a better way
for us to handle this situation

Let's Talk About It!

How Deep Is My Love

I wanna make your toes curl
or make you wanna grab ya thighs
as your hips gyrate in tune
with my every thrust of passion.

Dig ya nails into my back
screaming cries of joy
as exctasy explodes inside of you
from the sheer satisfaction.

Just to know ya man is serving you right
that's every woman's ultimate point of delight
taking you to a higher plane
where you've never been before.

Two sweat drenched souls
locked together like a vice grip
drained from this sensuous pain
but ya body's calling out for so much more.

That's the type of loving
that's sure to quench your thirst
and leave you fulfilled
as you close your eyes to sleep.

What a wonderful journey it is to take
with a man who understands
what his woman needs and wants
and whose love for you runs deep.

Strawberries 'N' Chocolate

All day I've been thinking about U
the taste in my mouth is the softness of your skin
What would I do without U
if we never made love again?

I like the taste of strawberries and whipped cream
dipped in your chocolate
The sweetness of your lips
makes my thoughts turn erotic

I'll never hunger for another
because you've quenched my thirst
U complete my soul
bring new life 2 me, like the Earth

In plentiful abundance
I extend my heart out to U
With U by my side
there's nothing I can't do

Touchin' Ya Self

Ain't no harm in a little self-stimulation
cause only U know your erogenous zones
Every woman has a itch that she needs to scratch
one night when she's home all alone

No man in your life
to treat U right
But your body's still jonesin'
for something kinky tonight

Put your hands in that place
that every man is not meant to see
Lay back, fantasize
imagine it was me

Caressing U slow
holding U close
Touching' Ya Self sometimes is the only way
to discover what excites U the most

Them Thighs, Them Thighs

A shapely, curvaceous figure
not too thick, but just right
Wrapped around my waist
in the heat of passion
the fit is so tight

Them Thighs, Them Thighs
they done mesmerized many men
Firm when U walk
the definition of every muscle
shows when U bend

Imagination running wild
the type of woman
to have my love child
69 different positions
I done peeped your profile

Undercover freak
with a ladylike disposition
Them Thighs, Them Thighs
they were made for kissing

Let Me Count The Ways

Let me think of some of the reasons
why I'm enchanted with U
Could it be your sweet smell, the way U walk
or just the things U do?

Maybe it's your smile
so radiant and bright
Warm thoughts fill my head
when I watch U sleep at night

I love the way U rub my shoulders
U can tell when I'm tense
Some things confuse me at times
but with U, it all makes sense

Your witty sense of humor
combined with intelligence that turns me on
Stimulating conversation
that keeps the love going strong

So many reasons I could reveal
but infinity is everlasting
U got me wrapped up in your love
sheer ecstasy and passion

My Best Friend

I love running my fingers
through your hair
Or kissing that soft spot
on the back of your neck

Every touch of your flesh against mine
is truly an adventure
A moment that I treasure
and never plan to forget

My Best Friend truly you are
the one who always offers comfort and support
I never have to worry cause you're always there
while so many others seem to fall so short

Straight up and down with me
just like when the clock strikes six o'clock
It's so many temptations for a man today
yet I know no other woman could take your spot

A diva in every way
but I know you got a little gangsta inside
Always there to hold me down
no matter how rough the ride

Bring The Love Back

As time passes on
and the nights grow long
I'm wondering to myself
how could I let you slip out of my life

If I could go back in time
and rewrite history
I swear this time
I would make things right

Throughout all of the confusion and
misunderstandings that we've had
It's so many things that were said
that today I know we both regret

Pleasant memories of what was
constantly possess my thoughts
Embedded images of you
which I just can't seem to forget

Lacking closure I lose my composure
every time I hear your name in conversation
It's got me hoping that it's not too late
for us to once again feel that calming sensation

Let's Bring the Love Back!

Moment Of Bliss

Marriage is the epitome
of God's destiny for humanity
Eternal love is forever
the end of selfish vanity

To share one's soul with another
is the manifestation of beneficence
A lifetime of commitment
the sacrifice is evident

When 2 combine as 1
in a fusion full of chemistry
A spontaneous combustion occurs
love is full of energy

Man and woman take a vow
to be united in bliss
A moment to be cherished by all
sealed with a kiss

Also available from the author

Reflections of My Soul:

A Collection

of Urban Poetry

ISBN No. 0-9715530-0-9
$9.99

This book is the author's first self-published title and consists of a collection of his most intimate poetry selections. There is at least one poem in this anthology that any reader can relate to in looking at his own personal life experiences or thoughts. Mr. Long gives us his personal outlook on issues such as urban life, intimate relationships, spirituality, and controversial social topics like HIV/AIDS, abortion, child abuse, and racism. All in all, this book is sure to be a delight for the intellectually inspired reader and a must have for anyone who finds inspiration in their lives from the spoken word.

To order your copy today or for additional copies of ***For My Sisters***, go to:

www.xslpublishing.com

Mail Order Page

Use this convenient order form to order additional copies of ***For My Sisters***

Please Print:

Name____

Address______________________________________

City______________________ **State**_______________

Zip________________ **Phone (   )**_______________

_____ copies of book @ $12.99 each $ ________

Postage and handling @ $ 3.50 per book $ ________

__ residents add __% tax $ ________

Total amount enclosed $ ________

Use this convenient order form to order additional copies of ***Reflections of My Soul***

Please Print:

Name____

Address______________________________________

City______________________ **State**_______________

Zip________________ **Phone (   )**_______________

_____ copies of book @ $ 9.99 each $ ________

Postage and handling @ $ 3.50 per book $ ________

__ residents add __% tax $ ________

Total amount enclosed $ ________

Mail to: XSL Publishing

c/o Thomas Long

P.O. Box 67192 • Baltimore, Maryland 21215